"Did I Ever Tell You About How Our Family Got Started?"

Deborah Shaw Lewis and Gregg Lewis

ZondervanPublishingHouse

Grand Rapids, Michigan

A Division of HarperCollinsPublishers

"Did I Ever Tell You About How Our Family Got Started?"
Copyright © 1994 by Deborah Shaw Lewis and Gregg Lewis

Zondervan Publishing House
Grand Rapids, Michigan 49530

Library of Congress Cataloging-in-Publication Data

Lewis, Deborah Shaw, 1951–
    "Did I ever tell you about how our family got started?" : building
togetherness and values by sharing stories about your family / by Deborah Shaw
Lewis and Gregg Lewis.
    p. cm. — (Family share together)
    ISBN 0-310-42111-X (softcover)
    1. Family—Anecdotes. 2. Marriage—Anecdotes. 3. Storytelling. 4. Family—
Folklore. 5. Oral biography. I. Lewis, Gregg A. II. Title. III. Series: Lewis,
Deborah Shaw, 1951– Family share-together book.
    HQ518.L48   1994   94-32862
    306.85—dc20   CIP

Illustrations by Liz Conrad

Printed in the United States of America

94 95 96 97 98 99 / ❖ CH / 6 5 4 3 2 1

Welcome to the Adventure of Storytelling!

Recently at our supper table, the subject of first kisses came up. I don't remember how the topic was introduced. I commented that I had no clear memory of the first time I kissed a boy. But I certainly remembered the first time I kissed Gregg.

I told the children that "fireworks" had gone off when he kissed me. Our children giggled. Our two teenage sons acted embarrassed. Five-year-old Jonathan wanted to know what fireworks we had been watching. But our children lost their embarrassed looks when they saw their father's face. Gregg laughed and blushed bright red and then redder, while I explained to Jonathan that by "fireworks" I meant that his father's kisses were wonderful—as exciting as fireworks. That I'd never felt that way when any other boy had kissed me. And that I still enjoy his father's kisses.

As I watched the laughing faces of my husband and children, I realized that we have told our children little about how Gregg and I met and dated and married. I don't remember ever showing our wedding album to the children. And now, as our two oldest sons are facing their dating years, those stories have an increased interest for them.

Because we have come to realize the importance and value of telling our children stories about our early adult years, we've included this book in our family storytelling series to encourage other parents to do the same. For your stories about how you, their parents, got together and how your individual family got started will interest your children and benefit them in numerous ways.

Such family stories could include the stories of your young adult days: career choices, spiritual decisions, and college days, as well as stories of how you and your spouse met, courted, and married.

We have discovered that when Gregg or I tell a story about that time in our lives, we give our children a new view of us as their parents—that we were once young adults, struggling with the life choices they will soon be making; that we were sometimes uncertain, sometimes mischievous, sometimes afraid, sometimes funny, sometimes lonely. As we tell about how our family began, they catch a glimpse of our past and a vision of their future.

In our culture, marked by mobility and the near-extinction of the extended family, such stories remind us of the significance of families and help our children understand the importance of relationships. They strengthen our roots and help us fill our need to belong.

In the past, most people learned life's important lessons from stories told at home. They heard stories of how their parents, grandparents, and other family members grew up, met and courted their spouses, got married, overcame problems, resolved conflicts, moved to new places, and started new families. In the hearing they gained a knowledge of their place in history.

Today, more and more families are abdicating that role to television. Too many of our children hear the stories of love and marriage, first kisses and blind dates, life choices and failures, only from strangers on a screen. Some kids can tell you much more about the fictional family history of the characters of their favorite show than they can about their own. Do we really want that for our children?

Family stories work two ways. They not only speak to our children about the family to which they belong, they also remind us parents of our own early adult years, our struggles with identity, our mischievous escapades, and the role God played in our life decisions. Furthermore, when we tell stories about how we met and married our mate, we remind ourselves, as well as our children, how much we love our spouse and what brought us together in the first place.

When we tell our children the stories about how God led us in our life choices—the jobs we held, the careers we pursued, and the schools we attended—we reaffirm those decisions. And we help instruct them in how to make such decisions for themselves.

Because each family begins in a different way and each family's history takes it own twists and turns, your family storytelling can be an exciting, enriching, and unpredictable adventure that will help you and your children discover a heritage uniquely your own. We encourage you to pursue that adventure with your family.

Maybe you're reading this and thinking, "I'm no storyteller! My kids wouldn't want to hear about that part of my life." Or "I wouldn't know where to start. Nothing remarkable or interesting ever happened in our family."

Then keep reading! For the rest of this book will be especially helpful for anyone who feels he or she has no family stories to tell.

While it may be true that most of us will never be great storytellers, every family has stories worth telling. And every child, as well as every parent, can benefit from stories about "How our family got started."

So we've designed the remainder of this book to help parents search their minds and memories to build a repertoire of stories from their early adult years. Our "Story Starters" and "Storytelling Tips" include a hodgepodge, bushel-basket full of story-related questions, suggestions, and comments to consider. You might want to think of them as a computer menu for calling up the files of your memory. Or as a set of keys for you to use to unlock the doors of your own rambling house of recollections.

Some entries on a computer menu are seldom used. A few keys on our old key rings no longer open any doors. In the same way, not all of the following material will effectively trigger your memories or elicit forgotten incidents. But some of them will. And when they do, when you start telling your children stories about "how our family got started," you will have begun your own great adventure of family storytelling.

*Tell about someone
you dated before
you met your spouse.*

- How did you meet him?
- How long did you go with him?
- How did you break up?
- In what ways was he like your husband or she like your wife?
- Now tell about your first boyfriend or girlfriend.

*Describe the first time
you remember seeing your spouse.*

- Where were you?
- What were you doing?
- What was your spouse doing?
- Did he or she see you, too?
- Were you introduced to each other? By whom?
- Did you talk to each other that day?
- What did you talk about?

> *When you look through these story questions, one incident in your life as a young adult will probably stand out in your memory: your first date with your spouse; an adventure you had as a young adult; or some other dramatic life event. That story is usually a good one to start with.*

Tell about the first time you asked your wife for a date.

- Did she say yes?
- Were you nervous about asking?
- How did you go about it?
- What do you remember about that first date?

Whenever you tell about an event or a person, set the story into a specific time and place. Begin with such details as, "I was eighteen years old when I met your father. I was a freshman at Asbury College, living in a dormitory room. Your dad was eighteen, too. He was living with his mom and dad, your Grandma and Grandpa, in the same house they live in now." Such details give the listener a framework for visualizing the setting for the story.

Story Starter

*Tell about a special date early
in your courtship with your spouse.*

- Where did you go and what did you do?
- What did you enjoy doing together?
- Tell about the first time you kissed your spouse.
- Describe a romantic date.
- Tell about a fight or disagreement you had while you were dating.
- Recount a date when your spouse did something that surprised you.

There are two sides to most of these stories. You and your spouse can take turns telling your version of each story, alternating back and forth in the telling. No two people remember the same event in the same way. Each of you will remember what was important to you. So expect your stories to differ, or even seem to conflict. Realize that neither memory is right or wrong, but it just comes from a different perspective.

Our First Date

This past Christmas we visited Gregg's parents, who still live where they lived while Gregg and I were dating. While we were there, it snowed. Grandpa and Uncle Mark got out sleds, and we all tramped over to where we could go sledding. There I told our children the story of our first date. This is an example of a full-blown story, one I have told my children on several occasions, and have thought through and dramatized.

The first time your daddy and I went out on a date, it was to go sledding on that hill over there, near where we are going today.

I first noticed your father when we had freshman biology class together. I even went back to the dorm and asked my friend Julia what she knew about "that boy named Gregg Lewis." Julia told me that he was a wonderful person, very athletic, really nice, but that he was going steady with a girl named . . . Donna . . . (*I drop my voice and make a face when I say her name*), someone he had known in high school. I was disappointed.

When we returned to college, the first day back after Christ-

mas break our freshman year, your daddy came over to the cafeteria to see me. And he asked me to go sledding with him that evening.

I went back to the dorm after work and found Julia again. Did she know? Had Gregg Lewis broken up with Donna? If he had, Julia didn't know about it.

Late that afternoon, Gregg picked me up at my dorm and we came to this hill—over here. He and I sledded down that hill and laughed and had a wonderful time. Uncle Mark and his girlfriend Martha sledded with us, using a second sled.

When I got too cold, we walked over to The Grill—the campus snack shop—and had hot chocolate together. I knew even then that I had never dated anyone else like Gregg Lewis. And I found out later, from Julia, that he had broken up with . . . Donna . . . over the Christmas holidays—because he wanted to ask me out.

My children laugh at that story. They think it's funny that their father once dated someone other than me. They love the way I drop my voice and frown when I say, "Donna." And they were, at first, surprised to realize that Uncle Mark dated someone named Martha before he married their Aunt Angela.

In his book *Seven Things Kids Never Forget* (Portland, Oregon: Multnomah Press, 1993) Ron Rose says, "Family stories help children find their place in the family, and they give children a solid sense of connection and belonging. And that linkage to others wards off the feelings of isolation and lack of accountability to others that can be so detrimental."

*When did you decide that you
wanted to marry your spouse?*

- What personality traits did you admire in him?
- What did you tell your friends or parents about him?
- Was there a specific time when you looked at him and thought, "This is the one I want to live with the rest of my life!" Tell about that time.

Each time we tell a story, the repetition jogs our memories and we remember another detail to add. Or we think of another way to fill out the story, to make it more dramatic, or to involve our children in the story.

Describe the time your husband asked you to marry him.

- Have him tell his side of the event.
- Tell about when you met your future in-laws.
- How did you tell your families about your engagement?
- How long were you engaged?

Details are important to make a story more interesting and colorful. Any details you remember add to the visual picture you give your child. You might describe what clothes you wore the day you proposed, or the car you drove at the time. Describe the weather and what time of day it was.

*Get out your wedding photographs
and look through them
with your children.*

- Tell a little about each picture.
- Who are the people in the photo and how did you know them?
- Why were they invited to the wedding?
- Tell about each of the wedding attendants.

As you are telling your children stories of your past, fill in the important details about the characters in the story. Make sure your children know names and ages. Look at these sentences: "I was twenty-one years old when your Daddy and I got married. And your cousin Lyn, who was one of the flower girls in our wedding, was eight years old then, and her brother Steven was five." Those details not only add to the story but also give children a frame of reference.

*Show your children pictures
from your honeymoon.
Tell them about that trip.*

- Where did you go and what did you see?
- Had either of you been there before?
- Now tell about another vacation or trip you took, just the two of you, in the first year or so of your marriage.
- Who did you visit or see on that trip?
- Now tell the story of the first time you and your spouse had to spend time apart.

As you tell the stories of your past, your children will naturally ask questions as a means of expressing interest. These questions may open up more details and more stories to tell. However, you should never feel pressured to answer a question that makes you feel uncomfortable. If such a question arises, simply say, "Let's leave that question for another time." And then move the conversation into a different direction.

*Describe the first house or
apartment the two of you
lived in after you were married.*

- In what town was it located? What was the address?
- How long did you live there?
- Imagine walking in the front door and describe what the place looked like.
- What family traditions began while you were living in that house or apartment?
- Describe a memorable meal fixed in that home.
- Tell about a time when you had visitors.

In our mind's computer, many of our memories are filed by the places in which they occurred. Remembering places is a powerful way to unlock the doors of our minds. As you tell your children about a place in your past, often the memories of events and people associated with that place will flow, as if a door has been opened. Out of those places and details, stories may grow.

*What was the first big purchase
you two made together?*

- What did you buy?
- How much did you pay for it?
- Did you save up for it?
- Describe the anticipation and the fulfillment of your plans.

> *Changing the pace of the story adds interest. Think of places where the telling should go faster or slower. Pause for dramatic effect at suspenseful parts of a story. Another way to add interest is the use of dramatic emphasis. In the story of our first date, I always say the name "Donna" with a frown and a scornful tone of voice. Any part of your story that lends itself to acting out, hand motions, or verbal emphasis makes the story that much more interesting for the listener. You can also use different voices for different people in your story.*

*Gather some photographs
from the early years
of your marriage.
Show them to your children
and tell about each one.*

Photograph albums are a wonderful way to jog your memory and illustrate some of the stories you tell. As you reminisce over the photos, your children will love to see pictures of you and your spouse as young adults, in college, or at your wedding. And, by looking through photographs, you will remember more stories to tell. Begin by answering these questions:

- Who are the people in the photo?
- How old were you or your spouse at the time?
- Was this taken before or after you were married?
- Tell the story illustrated by the photo.
- Tell what happened that is not shown here.

*Describe the first church
you attended as a couple.*

- What was the name of the church?
- Who was the pastor?
- How did you decide to attend that church?
- What denomination was it?
- Do you remember a sermon or Sunday school lesson you heard while attending that church?
- Tell about something funny—or memorable—you saw happen in that church.

*Tell the story of your first
big fight as a married couple.*

- What led up to the fight?
- How did each of you express your anger?
- How did you resolve the issue?
- Now tell about a time, that first year or so of your marriage, when you were proud of your mate.

Do not neglect to tell stories that are hard to tell. Stories of sadness and hardship give children a perspective beyond their own. They see how someone else faced troubles and triumphed, lived through sadness and found happiness again. Also tell stories about your mistakes, weaknesses, and failures. Those stories teach children what it means to be human. They can enable our listeners to really know us and allow us to feel truly known and loved. That's a big part of what belonging to a family is all about.

*Recall some big plan,
in the first year of your marriage,
that didn't turn out at all
the way you expected it to.*

- What did you have planned?
- What happened instead?
- Were you angry or upset at the turn of events, or did things work out better this way?
- How did each of you respond?

Family gatherings are good places to consult other family members. Your parents and brothers and sisters will have their own memories of meeting your spouse, of your dating years, or of your early jobs. There you can learn new family stories and fill in the details when your own memory is incomplete.

How did the two of you divide the responsibilities of a household?

- Which chores did your wife do?
- Which did your husband do?
- What job around the house did neither of you want to do?
- How did you make those decisions?
- Do you still divide those jobs in the same way?

> *My friend Susan grew up in a home where her father paid the monthly bills. Her husband Tom's mother handled that job. For the first three months of Susan and Tom's marriage, bills piled up, unpaid, in a basket, unnoticed in the initial adjustment to marriage and a new apartment. Each of them assumed the other was taking care of that business. A phone call from a collection agency finally brought the matter to their attention.*

*Did you ever lose
something that was
very important to your spouse?
Or break one of her possessions,
something that couldn't be fixed?*

If you want your kids to know you understand and empathize with a wide range of experiences and emotions, tell stories that reflect that range. Don't just recount the times and stories that show you in a good light. Also recall for them the times when you were the goat and really messed up. Let them hear about your disappointments as well as your proud moments.

Mama Knows How to Lose Keys

Sometimes I tell "grits" stories. On one storytelling tape, Kathryn Tucker Windham talks about her mother fixing grits every morning for breakfast. She recounts all the different ways grits could be fixed. She talks for five or six minutes about grits, and my children hang on her every word—laughing at the humorous lines. A "grits" story is a collection of interesting facts, thoughts, and memories about a subject. The subject here is my ability to lose car keys.

I have locked my keys in the car more times than I could possibly count!

One of the worst times was the day I took fifth graders from our church on a hike. This was after your daddy and I had been married for a year or so, and I had been teaching a Wednesday night group of fifth graders. They needed to go on a hike in order to earn a badge in hiking.

I had four fifth graders with me. We drove way out into this forest preserve west of Elgin, Illinois, where your daddy and I were living at that time. We had driven several miles from the last sign

of civilization in order to get to the head of this trail we were going to follow.

Well, we got out and got everyone's stuff out. And then I locked up the car.

It might not have been so bad if I had realized right away that my keys had been left in the car. But I didn't.

We went on our three-mile hike. We came back to the car, all tired and ready to get something to drink. But the drinks were in the car, and so were my keys.

So we took another hike, this time to the nearest house a mile or so away. At the house I called Gregg, but since we had only one car at the time, he had to call around and find someone who could drive him out to where we were. It seemed like forever before he got there with the keys. And, of course, those fifth graders never let me forget it.

The worst time I locked my keys in the car, though, may have been the time I left the motor running. That was the first week we lived in Illinois. We had driven up to Elgin the day before with

Uncle Mark, who was going to help us unpack and then drive the U-Haul truck back to Kentucky.

I left Gregg and his brother Mark unloading the truck and went to the grocery store. One of my favorite songs came on the radio as I was driving into the parking lot. I pulled into a parking place, put the car into park, but left the motor running while I listened to the end of the song. Then I jumped out of the car, locked the door, and ran into the store.

Thirty minutes later, I paid for my groceries and began to look for my keys. I couldn't find them. I walked out to the car to see if I had left the keys in it. As I walked out, I could hear that a car in the parking lot was running, really loud. As I got closer to our car, I got this sinking feeling. Surely, surely, I hadn't left the car running! But I had.

That car was so hot! I had to call Gregg, and he and Mark had to drive the moving truck to the grocery store with his set of the keys.

That is why I keep three sets of keys with me now. So, even if I lock the keys in the car, I always have a back-up set of keys in my purse.

*Describe the way you spent
a typical weekend in those
early days of your marriage.
Then tell the story of a weekend
that was different or special.*

Often as we remember stories of our past, we think only to describe what we saw. As you compile stories to tell your children about your young adult years, think about the other four senses too. What smell do you associate with each memory? Which sounds, especially music? How did something feel to the touch? What tastes or foods do you think of when you remember a person, place, or event of your past? Sensory details add texture and flavor to your stories. Try to include two or more kinds of sensory memories in every story you tell.

Tell the story of the first Christmas you spent together as a married couple.

- What Christmas gifts did you give each other?
- Where did you spend the holidays?
- Did you visit your parents? Tell about that visit.
- What Christmas traditions did you begin then?
- What did you do that you decided not to do again?
- Did you have a Christmas tree in your home? How did you decorate it?
- If you have photographs of that Christmas, show them to your children and tell about them.

Tell about the first birthday celebrations after you were married.

- What gift did your spouse give you for your birthday?
- Was it something you wanted?
- Did you have a party? Who was invited?
- What was memorable about that day?
- Was there another birthday celebration that was memorable?

Story Starter

*Tell the story of the day
you found out you were
going to have a child.*

- How long had you been married at that time?
- How did you tell your parents or other family members?
- Now tell the story of how you found out you were expecting each subsequent child.
- When you thought about having a family, what had you imagined?
- How many children did you think you would want to have?
- Did you have fertility problems? Tell about some of your feelings regarding that.

How Our Family Got Started

Here is a story we tell our children about our efforts to start a family.

When your daddy and I first got married, I dreamed about having children. I've always loved babies—always wanted to be a mother. And your daddy wanted to be a father. So after we had been married for three years, we decided it was time to start a family. But, as you know, your daddy and I were married six and a half years before Andrew was born.

When I didn't get pregnant after a while, we began to see doctors to find out what was wrong. We had two different fertility specialists tell us that we would probably never have children of our own.

We were seeing the second of those specialists when I got pregnant with Andrew. That doctor told us that Andrew was a "miracle."

One morning I was lying in bed playing with Andrew, who was about eleven months old. Your daddy was up and getting dressed for the day. And I felt a baby move inside me. There is no other feeling just like that. Who do you think I was feeling? (*Matthew*)

I went that day for a pregnancy test. That was July 8. We were thrilled when the test was positive—we had not expected a second miracle so soon!

Sometimes I think I'd like to go back and see that second fertility specialist and show her our family. Five children—and every one of you is a miracle.

In many ways, each of your children was born into a different family. How was your family different when each child came along?

- What were the different places where you lived when each of your children were born?
- How old were you at that time? How old were the siblings?
- How had your jobs, finances, or other circumstances changed by the time of each child's birth?

> *When our oldest son Andrew was born, our family lived in suburban Chicago, we had been married without children for almost seven years, Gregg was working as a full-time magazine editor, and I was working as a part-time college instructor. By the time our youngest son Jonathan was born, our family lived in the mountains of North Georgia, Gregg and I were both working as freelance writers at home, and Jonathan was the youngest of five children. The family into which each was born had a very different composition.*

*Tell about the first
full-time job you had.*

- How old were you?
- What work was involved?
- What did you enjoy about that job?
- How much money did you earn?
- Who were your friends at work?
- Does the work you do now have something in common with that first job?
- Did you learn something about yourself while doing that job?
- Tell about part-time jobs you've had.

Tell about the different towns or cities you have lived in.

- Did you live there before or after your marriage?
- What job did you work at while living there?
- What friends or roommates did you have there?
- What do you miss most about that time of your life?
- Tell about an adventure that happened while living there.

We have purposely focused our story-starter questions on the positive aspects of relationships and family life. But we are well aware that many of these questions may elicit powerful emotions for families that have suffered losses or divorce.

Even in such situations, your children will be interested in the stories of your young adult years and of your marriage. Storytelling may even be an effective means of opening up communication lines with your children regarding these sensitive issues.

What jobs did the two of you have when you were first married?

- How early in the morning did you leave for work?
- Describe your morning routine.
- Were the two of you able to eat breakfast, lunch, or dinner together?
- Who fixed the meals?
- Who arrived home first?
- What were your afternoon and evening routines?

*How did you decide on
the career, or job, you now have?*

- What events made you realize that you had the skills or aptitude for that job?
- What training or education did you need?
- What did you like, or not like, about that education?

Make eye contact with your children as you tell a story. Eye contact not only draws the audience in, it also keeps the teller in touch with the audience.

*Tell about a memorable person
you once worked with
or someone you once worked for.*

- Recount a time when you forgot an important appointment or blew an important assignment at work.
- Tell about a job you really hated.
- Describe an incident where a fellow worker lied to you, tricked you, or took credit for your work.
- Tell about a time when you succeeded at work and got the credit for it.

What was the most outrageous thing you did as a young adult?

- How old were you at the time?
- What made you decide to do what you did?
- Were you sorry afterwards?
- Who was with you?
- Who saw what you did?
- What happened as a result?
- Now tell about the most adventuresome thing you ever did.

If you can actively involve the listener in the story, you will add another element of interest. Two or three times during a story, you can stop and ask, "Can you imagine your father doing that?" Or ask any question that draws the listener into the story.

Story Starter

Looking back, what was the most dangerous thing you remember doing? Or the most dangerous situation you found yourself in?

- What were the circumstances of that day?
- Who was with you? Were they in danger, too?
- Were you frightened? Did you realize what danger you were in?
- How did you get out of danger? Were you hurt or injured?
- What happened after the incident was over?

Story Starter

*When you were a young adult,
were you ever seriously ill
or injured in an accident?
Tell about that time in your life.*

- Was this before or after your marriage?
- Were you hospitalized?
- What lasting effects did the illness have?
- Who took care of you? Do you remember a doctor or nurse from that time?

Family storytelling is more than just an effective means of communicating family values and of helping our children think about the choices they will make as teenagers and young adults. It is a gift you give your children. Each time you tell a family story, you have given them your time and attention, and a piece of yourself. And your children can pass that gift on to their children.

*Tell about a day
that changed your life.*

- How old were you? Was this before or after your marriage?
- Did you have a decision to make?
- How was your life different after this day?
- Did those changes make you happy or sad?
- Describe one of the spiritual milestones in your life. If you're a Christian, tell about the day you made a personal commitment to Christ.

Everyone has days that are critical points in their lives. At some turning places, a decision must be made: who to marry; what career to pursue; if and where to go to college; whether or not to move. For Christians this includes their decision to follow God. Sometimes the turning point is something out of our control: we are fired from our job; someone we love dies; we are involved in a serious automobile accident. These days are crucial to who we are, and they stand out in our memory. Stories about such crucial days help the listeners understand how we became the people we are today.

Aunt Mary

Don't neglect to tell the stories that are difficult to tell: the stories of sadness or failure. Such stories show children the full range of life's experiences. What follows is the story of a day of sadness when I made a difficult life choice.

When I was growing up, I thought my mother was the most beautiful woman in the world. But I thought my aunt Mary was the most glamorous.

Looking back I marvel at that. Aunt Mary was a poor mill worker. She dipped snuff and lived in a small mill-shack house. But all I saw of her was that she had bright red hair and big blue eyes. Her hair was the color of Benjamin's and her eyes were big and blue like his, too. When she dressed up, she wore fashionable clothes. At least she seemed glamorous to the eyes of a small child who loved her.

And I did love Aunt Mary. She loved children and always had time for us. She always had nickles and candy in her pocket to give to us when we visited her.

I remember the day she married my uncle Pearce. I was only

four or five years old. She had been married before, but her first husband, whom I never knew, died in an accident.

I can close my eyes and still see the way she looked that day. She was wearing a green, smartly tailored suit that looked so sophisticated. It contrasted with her red hair. I thought she could have been a model!

Even on her wedding day, she found time to get down on my level, look right at me, and talk to me.

I loved my aunt Mary.

Now memories are funny things. I know that in the years following that day, we visited my aunt Mary on a regular basis. She lived with Mama Baird, and then across the street from Mama Baird. And I remember playing in her yard. She still had nickles—and time—for the children. I know she must have aged, gained weight, changed.

But my visual memory was still that picture of her, standing on the porch of Mama Baird's house, dressed in that stylish green suit, red hair bright in the sun, slender, smiling, and attractive.

Until the day we visited her when I was a senior in high school.

I think her marriage to Uncle Pearce was not a happy one. She loved children, but she never had children of her own. I think that made her unhappy, too. And Uncle Pearce drank a lot. I imagine that, at first, she started drinking to keep him company.

I think, too, that my parents tried to protect us from knowing about the changes in Aunt Mary's life. I knew that Mama Baird had moved across the street. But I didn't know that she did that because Aunt Mary and Uncle Pearce were drinking too much.

When we visited Mama Baird, there were times when we just didn't see Aunt Mary, even though she lived across the street.

So, for whatever the reasons, I have only the two visual memories of Aunt Mary. The way she looked on her wedding day. And the way she looked that day my senior year.

We were standing in front of Mama Baird's house that day when Aunt Mary walked over to see us. She was wearing a worn print dress. Food had dribbled down the front and dried. She wore two mismatched socks, one of which was rolled down. She had washed her face and tried to comb her beautiful red hair. But she hadn't been sober enough to comb the back of her hair. She had only brushed out what she could see in the mirror. The back of her hair was a matted mess that stuck out in all directions.

Her big beautiful blue eyes had always gotten down on my level and focused in on me. But on this day they were tired, dim, not quite focused on anything.

She had gargled with Evening in Paris perfume to disguise the smell of alcohol on her breath. That is probably the worst smell in the world—the smell of beer mixed with Evening in Paris perfume.

As we stood in front of my grandmother's house and talked, I opened my eyes and, for the first time in years, saw my aunt Mary as she was, rather than as I remembered her from earlier years.

All my life I had heard my parents talk about "the evils of alcohol." About how many people had ruined their lives with it. About how alcoholics lose themselves to their drink. And about how "No Shaw or Baird has ever been able to drink and live a sober life."

That day was the first time I understood what they meant.

There, in front of my eyes, was someone I loved, lost in that fog of alcoholism. Lost to us as well as to herself.

And with a fear that made it hard for me to breathe, I realized my own risk. I came from a family with a strong hereditary risk for alcoholism. Standing in front of me was a clear example of what I could be.

All the way home that day, I stared out the window of the car. I grieved over the loss of the Aunt Mary who had simply not been there that day. And, over and over, in my head, I said to myself, "Not me. I will never take that risk with my life. Not me."

In all the years since, at all the parties where I might have had a beer or a glass of wine, I have never even wanted to. In fact, even now, more than thirty years after that day, the smell of alcohol brings back that memory as if it were yesterday. A whiff of beer and I see Aunt Mary's face—I even smell Evening in Paris perfume, mixed with beer.

*If you could pick
one day in your life
that you could live over again,
what day would you pick?*

- If you could pick one day that you could live over again, and be able to change what you did that day—or something that happened that day—what day would you pick? Tell about that.

Family stories help our children realize the significance of individual lives, both their own and their parents'. In today's "global community," we are exposed to constant media portrayals of famous people and their accomplishments: from presidents to rock stars; from superstar athletes to jet-setting billionaires. These are the people our world deems "significant." In comparison to the people who make the headlines, we often think of ourselves as insignificant. Young people in particular feel overwhelmed by their personal lack of power and influence. Family stories remind them that in God's plan they and their parents have a special place.

*Tell the story of the day
God answered a prayer for you
in a way you would never
have imagined.*

Do not wait until your story is "perfect" to tell it. Most of us stumble around a bit as we tell a story for the first time. Children are very forgiving audiences. Don't wait to be a "great storyteller," either. According to Sylvia Ziskind, author of *Telling Stories to Children* (H.W. Wilson, 1976): "Everybody likes to tell a story. Little children do it effortlessly. Great artists do it with native talent and years of practice. Somewhere in between stand you and I."

Recount a time when you lost someone you loved.

- How old were you when he died? How old was he?
- What do you remember of the funeral?
- Tell about a good memory you have of that person.

When Gregg and I had been married eight months, my grand-mother died. It was early December and we had been planning to travel home for Christmas. We didn't have the money for me to fly home for the funeral, and also go home again for the holidays. I chose not to attend the funeral. Even now, twenty years later, thoughts of that choice bring tears to my eyes.

*Tell about the time
you served in the military.*

- Which branch of the service? When?
- Tell about the day you left home for the service.
- What was boot camp like?
- Tell about your war experiences.
- Remember the day you came home.
- In what ways did your military experience change your life?

Another way to come up with family stories is to listen to some of the experts. Our family has acquired several audio tapes of master storytellers Donald Davis and Kathryn Tucker Windham, both of whom tell family stories. Listening to both of these talented story-tellers has given us story ideas and shown us ways to enhance our own accounts of personal experiences.

*Tell us about leaving home
for the first time to go to college.*

- What college did you attend?
- How did you decide to go there? Were you far from home?
- Was this the first time you lived away from your parents' home?
- Show your children photos of your college days.
- How old were you when you started college?
- What do you remember about the first day? That first year?
- Describe the dormitory or other housing where you lived.
- Who was your roommate?
- Did you belong to a fraternity or sorority? Tell about that.

> *The more stories you tell, the more stories you will remember. Usually telling one story will remind you of another to work on. Sometimes a story is brought to mind by something your child says or does, or a situation that you or someone in your family faces today.*

Tell about a time as a young adult when you got into trouble.

My Brother's Middle-of-the-Night Visit

Many of the stories I tell our children about our years as young adults are on-the-spot stories—anecdotes I stumble through as the occasion arises. Sometimes they develop into stories that are told again and again.

Last summer Gregg and I attended our college twenty-year reunion. While there, I walked around the college campus with our children, telling them one story after another of our days there. One was the story of the night my brother Terrell sneaked me out of the dorm.

Asbury College was very strict about their rules when your daddy and I went there. We had to be in the dormitory early—by ten o'clock on week nights. Once the doors were locked we were not allowed out. And boys were certainly not allowed in the girls' dorms, except in the parlor. And not even in the parlor after hours.

Now, Uncle Terrell also went to Asbury. But he graduated in June of 1969, and I started in the fall of 1969. So we were never in school there at the same time.

After Terrell graduated, he taught in the Teacher Corps, which was a government program that recruited teachers for poorer areas of the country. He was teaching in West Virginia. And he came back to Asbury that fall, after he graduated. He came to see me—but also to visit his friends who were still in college there.

He got on campus really late—after eleven that night. And he got someone to let him into Glide-Crawford dormitory. I don't know who let him in. All I know is that someone came down to my room and told me that my brother was in the parlor.

I came out and talked to him for a little while. And then he said he was hungry. Would I like to drive with him into Nicholasville and get something to eat?

I knew that leaving the dorm after hours was breaking the rules. But I was a first-quarter freshman, and had no idea how much trouble I would have gotten into if we had been caught. The college would have treated our little adventure very seriously! I would almost certainly have been called before the discipline committee.

We walked out of the dorm and got into Terrell's car, as if it were no big deal. We drove to a late-night restaurant and had a

good time talking. He told me all about the Teacher Corps and West Virginia. And I told him how I was doing my first quarter. He gave me all kinds of advice about college.

Terrell had always been my big brother. That night was the first time I remember talking to him as an equal.

When we drove back to the campus, it was after midnight. He tried the back door of the dorm. It was locked. For the first time, Terrell seemed nervous—as if it would matter if we were seen by the night watchman. And suddenly I began to think about the rules—and how I might get into trouble with the college authorities.

We walked around to one side of the dorm, and Terrell threw little pebbles against one of the windows. Autumn Creeks, one of his old girlfriends, came to the window. When she saw who it was, she slipped down and unlocked a back door for me.

I said good-bye and went on to bed. That was the first time—but by no means the last—that I slipped in or out of that dorm. And in four years of college, I never once got caught.

I didn't mean disrespect for the college. I really didn't. I was just accustomed to a lot more independence. My mama and daddy—your grandmother and granddaddy—had allowed me to drive and go places on my own. My senior year of high school, I drove into Atlanta alone to go to the library there, more times than I can count. So going and doing things on my own, without signing in or out, seemed like the right thing to do at the time.

As I told that story to my children, twenty-some years after the fact, I shuddered. How would I react if one of my children were caught breaking the rules, the way I did as a college student? That day was the first time I had ever thought about those escapades as a parent, rather than a college student.

Story Starter

What extracurricular activities were you involved in during your college years?

- Were you involved in the band? Drama? The college newspaper? Choir? Student government? Tell about those experiences.
- Did you play college sports? Which sport? What position?
- Who else was a part of that extracurricular activity? Were any of them your friends?
- Tell about how you spent your Christmas vacations or summer breaks from college.

*Who was your favorite
singer or musician?*

- Did you ever see her in person? Or attend one of her concerts? Tell about that day.
- What were your favorite songs?
- What movies did you see when you were in your late teens and early twenties? Which ones were your favorites? What do you remember about them?
- Did you have a favorite major league baseball player or team? Who did you root for? Tell us about a visit to a major league game.

Describe the first car you owned.

- What was the make and model?
- How did you acquire the car?
- Where did you go in that car?
- Tell about a specific trip, or day, in that vehicle.
- Describe another vehicle you owned.

> *When we tell our children family stories, we can re-discover a powerful means of communicating with the next generation. Stories reach past our minds and into our hearts. They bring our children up close, into the situation, so they feel the feelings and identify with the story's characters. Stories can bypass misunderstandings or hurt feelings and bridge the gap between listener and teller.*

*Tell your children
what you remember about
the day men first walked
on the moon.*

Now pick one of these historical events and tell how it impacted your life. What do you remember about:

- The day President John Kennedy was shot.
- The day Dr. Martin Luther King was killed.
- The day the U.S. pulled out of Vietnam.
- The day John Lennon was shot.
- The day Hank Aaron hit the home run that broke Babe Ruth's record.
- The explosion of the Challenger.
- Watching the Berlin wall come down.
- The break-up of the Soviet Union.
- The first presidential candidate you voted for and why.

"Did I Ever Tell You About . . ."

This past summer at a weekend reunion of Gregg's extended family, we sat around a campfire one evening with his parents, his brothers, three sets of aunts and uncles, and more than a dozen cousins, taking turns telling stories about how we'd all met, dated, and married our spouses. As we talked, listened, and laughed into the night, I noticed several teenage members of the family had joined the circle and were listening with interest to these abridged tales of love and romance related by the older generations of the family. And I thought, *What a wonderful way for our kids to learn some important lessons about love and marriage!*

But we shouldn't need a big family reunion to help us remember and share with our children the important experiences of our young adulthood that brought us and them to the point where we are today. For family storytelling has traditionally taught family values and family identity.

Admittedly, the other three books in this series may present a simpler challenge. It's probably easier for us to tell our children stories about our own childhood, about their grandparents, or about their own earlier years. The questions posed here may force us to dig a little deeper emotionally. But our own family experience with storytelling convinces us the effort is well worth it.

We trust that as you have been reading this book, you have begun experimenting with telling your children stories about "How Our Family Got Started."

One nice thing about a list of questions like we've included in this book is that you can use it again and again with different results. A quick one-time read-through may trigger one layer of especially memorable stories. If you do the same thing again a month from now, your mind will make some new memory connections. And if you really take some time and pick just two or three questions to focus your brainstorming, you'll often uncover additional levels and experiences that you didn't remember the first time through.

And as you use this book, we hope you have lots of fun. Because family storytelling should be enjoyable—both for you and for your children. If it's not fun, slow down. It takes time for stories to come together, for families to develop the habit of telling stories.

As you tell family stories to your children, it will indeed become a habit, woven into the very fabric of your relationships with each other. Your children will think to ask for family stories more often. And you'll find yourself regularly asking, "Did I ever tell you about . . ."

Enter the Creating Family Memories Contest!

Do you have a family story to share? It could get you published! Or send you on a family vacation of a lifetime!

Here's How. Write out your favorite family story and mail it to the address below. Your story will be judged on its originality and on how well the event created a lasting memory or drew your family together. The story must be original and not previously published, typed or neatly handwritten, and 500 words or less.

The Prizes. The ten best stories will be published in *Christian Parenting* ($100 value). Grand prize is a six-day, five-night family vacation for four to anywhere in the continental United States. The contest is cosponsored by USAir and Holiday Inn.

Mail in your story with your name, address, and phone number to: Creating Family Memories, Attn. Betty Wood B16, Zondervan Publishing House, Grand Rapids, MI 49530.

The Official Rules. No purchase necessary. Ten winners will be published in *Christian Parenting* magazine ($100 value). One grand prize consists of six days, five nights at a Holiday Inn, round-trip airfare on USAir, rental car, and $200 spending money, for a total $2,500 value. No cash substitute. Entries must be received by March 31, 1995. Judging will be conducted by a panel, and its decisions shall be final. Sponsor not responsible for lost or damaged mail. Taxes are winners' responsibility. All entries become the property of sponsor. The contest is open to residents of the United States, 21 years and older. All prizes will be awarded. Employees or their family members of Zondervan, Family Bookstores, HarperCollins, or their advertising affiliates may not enter. A list of prize winners may be obtained after July 31, 1995 by sending a self-addressed, stamped envelope to the address listed above.